IMAGES OF WAR

7TH SS MOUNTAIN DIVISION PRINZ EUGEN AT WAR 1941-1945

RARE PHOTOGRAPHS FROM WARTIME ARCHIVES

Ian Baxter

Pen & Sword
MILITARY

First published in Great Britain in 2019 by
PEN & SWORD MILITARY
An imprint of
Pen & Sword Books Ltd
47 Church Street
Barnsley
South Yorkshire
S70 2AS

ISBN 978-1-52672-142-6

A CIP catalogue record for this book is available from the British Library.

Typeset by Concept, Huddersfield, West Yorkshire HD4 5JL.
Printed and bound in India by Replika Press Pvt. Ltd.

Pen & Sword Books Limited incorporates the imprints of Atlas, Archaeology, Aviation, Discovery, Family History, Fiction, History, Maritime, Military, Military Classics, Politics, Select, Transport, True Crime, Air World, Frontline Publishing, Leo Cooper, Remember When, Seaforth Publishing, The Praetorian Press, Wharncliffe Local History, Wharncliffe Transport, Wharncliffe True Crime and White Owl.

For a complete list of Pen & Sword titles please contact
PEN & SWORD BOOKS LIMITED
47 Church Street, Barnsley, South Yorkshire S70 2AS, England
E-mail: enquiries@pen-and-sword.co.uk
Website: www.pen-and-sword.co.uk

Contents

About the Author

Ian Baxter is a military historian who specialises in German twentieth-century military history. He has written more than fifty books including *Poland – The Eighteen Day Victory March*, *Panzers In North Africa*, *The Ardennes Offensive*, *The Western Campaign*, *The 12th SS Panzer-Division Hitlerjugend*, *The Waffen-SS on the Western Front*, *The Waffen-SS on the Eastern Front*, *The Red Army at Stalingrad*, *Elite German Forces of World War II*, *Armoured Warfare*, *German Tanks of War*, *Blitzkrieg*, *Panzer-Divisions at War*, *Hitler's Panzers*, *German Armoured Vehicles of World War Two*, *Last Two Years of the Waffen-SS at War*, *German Soldier Uniforms and Insignia*, *German Guns of the Third Reich*, *Defeat to Retreat: The Last Years of the German Army At War 1943–45*, *Operation Bagration – the Destruction of Army Group Centre*, *German Guns of the Third Reich*, *Rommel and the Afrika Korps*, *U-Boat War*, and most recently *The Sixth Army and the Road to Stalingrad*. He has written over a hundred articles including 'Last days of Hitler', 'Wolf's Lair', 'The Story of the V1 and V2 Rocket Programme', 'Secret Aircraft of World War Two', 'Rommel at Tobruk', 'Hitler's War With his Generals', 'Secret British Plans to Assassinate Hitler', 'The SS at Arnhem', 'Hitlerjugend', 'Battle of Caen 1944', 'Gebirgsjäger at War', 'Panzer Crews', 'Hitlerjugend Guerrillas', 'Last Battles in the East', 'The Battle of Berlin', and many more. He has also reviewed numerous military studies for publication, supplied thousands of photographs and important documents to various publishers and film production companies worldwide, and lectures to various schools, colleges and universities throughout the United Kingdom and the Republic of Ireland.

Introduction

Drawing on a superb collection of rare and unpublished photographs, this book is the 7th in the Waffen-SS Images of War series by Ian Baxter. The 7th SS Mountain Division was a German volunteer mountain division which was formed in 1941 from the *Volksdeutsche*, ethnic German volunteers and conscripts from the Banat, the independent state of Croatia, Hungary, and Romania. It fought a counter insurgency campaign against communist-led Yugoslav partisan resistance forces in occupied Serbia and Montenegro. With in-depth captions and text the book describes its recruitment, organisation and training, from its first beginnings leading a German-Bulgarian anti-guerrilla offensive in Serbia against the Chetniks to its evolution into a fully-fledged Waffen-SS division fighting and murdering its way across the Balkans. It describes how it operated against partisan activity in Yugoslavia where it fought a series of vicious actions alongside both the German and Italian armies. For three years the division undertook a series of bloody anti-partisan operations where it often murdered local civilians and left villages burned or destroyed.

During the final months of the war in the Balkans the division went on the defensive against Soviet forces in Bulgaria, where it fought until its units were either destroyed or had withdrawn into Slovenia, where it surrendered to Yugoslavian forces.

The book provides much information and many facts about the division, the weapons, the uniforms it wore, and its battle tactics. It provides a captivating glimpse into one of the most brutal groups of soldiers ever assembled in military history.

* * *

All images credited as NARA are from US The National Archives and Records Administration.

Chapter One

Formation

On 6 April 1941 the German invasion of Yugoslavia and Greece began. The first attacks into Yugoslavia began with the bombing of Belgrade. Simultaneously on the ground, the German 2nd Army (with elements of the 12th Army, First Panzer Group, and an independent panzer corps) attacked. In total there were nineteen divisions, including five panzer divisions, two motorised infantry divisions and two mountain divisions. The attack was overwhelming for the weak and undertrained Yugoslav army and conditions further deteriorated with the Italian and Hungarian Army joining the ground offensive on 11th April.

In spite of the devastating blow, the Yugoslavian people were determined to resist. In a number of areas the countryside was inflamed by local uprisings, and partisan groups began attacking German convoys. Even after the capitulation of Yugoslavia, faction groups began calling on the people to unite in a battle against the occupiers. Many Serb detachments that had refused to surrender to the Germans had taken to the hills. The Chetniks, or what they referred to sometimes as 'Chetnik detachments of the Yugoslavian Army', were the first of the two main resistance movements. The Chetniks were composed mostly of Serbs soldiers, local defence units, bands of Serb villagers, anti-partisan auxiliaries, mobilised peasants and armed refugees. All were intent on retaining the Yugoslav monarchy, ensuring the safety of ethnic Serb people, and the establishment of a Great Serbia. The other partisan movement, however, which was led by the communist leader Josip Broz Tito, was regarded as anti-Serbian. Yet it largely cooperated in their anti-Axis activities with Chetnik leaders, actively recruiting partisans that fought side-by-side with Tito's insurgents.

Brutal guerrilla warfare broke out in 1941 in many parts of Yugoslavia. The deep forests, mountains, hills and valleys, became plagued with guerrilla activities. Partisan detachments began infiltrating enemy lines with snipers firing on German convoys. They put some whole regions in a state of war. Bridges were blown, roads were blocked with tree trunks or wagons, or were mined. Special Partisan detachments severed lines of communications, sabotaging railways and assaulting enemy supply dumps. Squads were dispatched to poison water wells.

Jittery German soldiers often over-reacted. If shots were fired at them from a village in bandit country, houses were torched, villages razed, and the inhabitants, innocent as well as guilty, found themselves facing firing squads. In towns and villages that had seen action against the Partisans, angry files of German soldiers marched through streets, hammering on doors, ordering out their petrified inhabitants and herding them out into the streets. Almost invariably the Germans would murder them in the most abominable fashion.

The indiscriminate killing of women, children and the elderly led to an increase in Partisan activity. Both sides fought savagely. It was a hidden war, unseen by judging eyes, and became dirty and ruthless in the extreme.

To combat the growing partisan issue the higher SS and police leader in Serbia, SS-Obergruppenführer August Meyszner, was issued with the task of putting together a volunteer division. Initially some were recruited from German-speaking Danube Swabia in the Banat region. However, the numbers did not reach an operating strength, so the SS discarded a voluntary recruiting programme and imposed a mandatory military recruitment scheme on all German-speaking people in Croatia and the Banat. This conscription programme was the first of its kind to non-Germans and the recruits were unable to oppose it.

Unlike the premier Waffen-SS divisions now fighting on the Eastern Front, the recruits were not expected to meet very stringent criteria. During their training programme new recruits were not indoctrinated to fight for the Führer, but to cleanse the Balkans from the Partisans. But every man had to obey every order, even if it meant shooting prisoners and committing atrocities against civilians. Under Meyszner's supervision, this new band of men learnt to be brutal.

In March 1942 the division declared itself a mountain division and was named the SS Freiwilligen Gebirgs Division, and a month later received the honorary title 'SS Prinz Eugen'.

Each soldier was trained hard and learnt the harshness of the environment in which he had to operate. He had to carry considerable personal kit, and was expected to scale mountains carrying it. The support elements that were available to traditional infantry divisions, such as armoured vehicles, tanks and artillery, were not supposed to be used by the mountain troops. Instead, they were supplied with weapons and other equipment that could be taken apart and carried by pack animals, just like a regular mountain trooper or *Gebirgsjäger*. The division's weapons consisted of a considerable number of non-standard weapons such as used captured French light tanks and Czech ZB-53 machine guns. However, the men did receive German artillery such as the 7.5cm Gebirgshaubitze 36 and the 10.5cm Gebirgshaubitze 40.

Each soldier had to learn survival techniques for the mountains. He was trained to build a primitive shield of rocks around him, which could protect him against the cold and enemy fire. The mountain soldiers became self-sufficient and adapted to mountain warfare.

Pictured here with SS Reichsführer Heinrich Himmler is SS Obergruppenführer August Meyszner, who can be seen standing up chairing the meeting. Meyszner was described as one of Himmler's most brutal subordinates. He held the post of Higher SS and Police Leader in Serbia, and in 1942 was issued with the task of putting together a volunteer division. This division became later known as the SS Prinz Eugen Division. (NARA)

A portrait photograph of SS Obergruppenführer Artur Phleps. It was Phleps who in March 1942 raised the new SS Freiwilligen Division Prinz Eugen. During his time with them, he was referred to as 'Papa Phleps' by his men.

Himmler seen disembarking from his aircraft warmly greeting a saluting SS Obergruppenführer August Meyszner before SS Prinz Eugen forces commenced operations in Serbia in 1942.

Himmler is pictured during a visit to units of the SS Prinz Eugen Division at a training ground. This division was formed in 1941 from the Volksdeutsche (ethnic German) volunteers and conscripts from the Banat, Independent State of Croatia, Hungary, and Romania. Himmler intended that this new division would be used in a counter-insurgency campaign against communist-led Yugoslav Partisan resistance forces in the occupied areas of Serbia and Montenegro. (NARA)

Himmler seen during an SS Prinz Eugen military exercise. *(NARA)*

(**Above**) Here is a Prinz Eugen officer cuff title worn on the sleeve by NCOs serving in the units of the 7th SS. It was made from silver thread on a black woven wool base with aluminium silver wire border.

(**Below**) Himmler photographed with commanders watching troops moving an artillery piece during a training exercise. (*NARA*)

(**Opposite, above**) SS soldiers at their barracks before a training exercise. The recruits of SS Prinz Eugen were not expected to meet the very stringent criteria that the premier Waffen SS divisions had to. During their training programme new recruits were not indoctrinated to fight for the Führer but to cleanse the Balkans from the Partisans. They had to obey every order, even if it meant shooting prisoners and committing atrocities against civilians.

(**Opposite, below**) A soldier cleaning his Karabiner 98K bolt action rifle in the spring of 1942 in Yugoslavia. His Zeltbahn shelter has been erected for use as a place to sleep.

During initial operations in Yugoslavia, pictured here is an SS Prinz Eugen base camp comprising tents and Zeltbahn shelter quarters. These field tents were of standard design and had a fly sheet to protect from rain and insulate from the sun's heat. They were quick to set up and take down.

At another base camp is a number of vehicles including two prime mover halftracks. These halftracks were mainly used to tow heavy ordnance such as 10.5cm and 15cm howitzers from one part of the front to another. SS Prinz Eugen seldom used such heavy guns as they were not practical in the often hilly areas of Yugoslavia.

A motorcycle combination has halted on an alpine road with another motorcyclist wearing his distinctive motorcycle leathers, probably waiting to clamber into the sidecar. These troops are more than likely part of a mountain reconnaissance battalion which consisted of a staff, a motorcycle company, and a heavy company.

A mountain troop column using animal draught crosses a muddy field during operations in Yugoslavia in 1942. These soldiers are hauling 3.7cm PaK35/36 guns. Even though the PaK35/36 had become inadequate for operational needs in the face of growing armoured opposition, they were still capable of causing serious damage to their opponent.

(**Opposite, above**) Gebirgs troops during operations in Yugoslavia in 1942. Roads were infested with partisans, making marching dangerous for the Germans and hindering their advance.

(**Opposite, below**) Troops crossing one of the bridges that linked the Serbian hills. Marching was often slow, and carrying heavy equipment almost impossible.

(**Above**) Regular troops pause during their march in Yugoslavia.

(**Above**) Gebirgs troops in a forest. The company commander can be seen kneeling next to an MG34 machine gunner. Apart from the commander, all the men are wearing the Zeltbahn. The Zeltbahn was designed with a slit in the middle for the wearer's head and could be worn comfortably over the shoulders hanging down to protect the army field service uniform and field equipment. When worn like this the Zeltbahn was known as the *Regenmantel* or rain cape.

(**Opposite, above**) An artillery unit during a pause in action. The artillery piece, well concealed in undergrowth, is a 10.5cm le.FH.18 light field howitzer.

(**Opposite, below**) Two motorcycle combinations have halted near some stationary prime mover halftracks that are hauling 15cm field howitzers. The 15cm field howitzer was primarily designed to attack targets deep into the enemy rear. A heavy mountain gun battery usually comprised three batteries fielding the 15cm howitzer, although they were cumbersome in mountainous areas.

Three photographs taken in sequence showing a motorcycle combination crossing a light wooden pontoon bridge known by the Germans as a Brückengerät 'C' type bridge. It appears still to be under construction as pioneers can still be seen on the bridge working. Note the pontoon boats held in place by ropes attached to the river bank.

Motorcyclists negotiate a churned-up road in 1942. Motorcyclists were used for dispatch purposes, being able to move swiftly across varied terrain.

SS Prinz Eugen soldiers pause in the summer heat. One man can be seen drinking beer beneath an improvised piece of Zeltbahn shelter. The division was not properly operational until October 1942 when it went into action against Tito's partisans.

Chapter Two

Anti-Partisan Operations

By the time the mountain division was assigned to the Balkans as an anti-partisan mountain division, German military operations on the Eastern Front were already well underway. Late 1941 had seen the first snowfall along the German front. With no preparations made for winter warfare, the German army nearly froze to death. By the beginning of the summer in May 1942, a new offensive was unleashed on the southern front bringing new hope to the German army. However, once again, the Wehrmacht met opposition, engaging in a protracted urbanized war inside the smouldering city of Stalingrad.

The drain on men and materials to the Eastern Front had a huge impact on the supply of troops in the Balkans, and through 1942 the German government were hard pressed to deal with the drastic increase in guerrilla activity. To make matters worse, the fact that the Bulgarian government had been forced into a war by Germany had so angered the Bulgarian people that a united underground Bulgarian Communist Party was formed. This led to widespread anti-partisan activity in Bulgaria including resistance movements called the Fatherland Front, the Zveno movement, and a number of other guerrilla factions too.

To deal with the partisan problems in Yugoslavia and Bulgaria, the German mountain division, together with the German and Bulgarian armies, were assigned to a large scale clearing offensive. This included clearing Chetniks in the Kopaonik, Jastrebac and Goc mountains, and the operation was aimed at destroying the Rasina Corps of the Yugoslav army.

In the spring of 1942, the SS Prinz Eugen Mountain Division was given orders to attack the Chetnik forces in northern Serbia as these partisans were causing problems to the road network and delaying the movement of valuable war materials which were needed to sustain the German war effort in North Africa through the Morava-Vardar valley.

Although liberation from the Germans seemed far away and the German hold on the Balkans still appeared unshakeable, the partisans were as determined as ever to resist. However, the local population paid a terrible price in reprisals. Civilians who lived near the sites of ambushes were routinely seized and shot.

The Germans were aware that they did not control large areas of countryside. Assault forces attacking guerrilla-held areas often had no knowledge of the terrain in which they were operating, and sometimes had to be led by local guides. In dense forests, deep valleys or ravines, or advancing through mountainous areas, radio or telephone links were often broken, and this meant that each company fought with no means of judging the progress of others, regularly isolating groups of soldiers and making them vulnerable.

Through 1942 partisans continued their campaign against the Germans across northern Serbia, energetically attacking convoys, trains, rail links and roads. The lack of adequate transport coupled with the substantial distances in unfavourable terrain caused the SS logistical problems, in spite the support of Bulgarian forces. Fuel supplies were a major concern and the crippling of rail lines coming into Yugoslavia prevented additional supplies from being received. Local German, Bulgarian and SS posts and garrisons were regularly surrounded, and sometimes even besieged. To regain control, the SS Prinz Eugen was ordered to destroy every vestige of opposition, even if it meant killing women and children.

In early October 1942 the division was ranked seventh in the order of battle of the Waffen-SS. Although a conscript division, volunteer in name only, it was firmly believed that being placed as the 7th SS division would give it a feeling of moral authority.

Around the same time, the new 7th SS Division 'Prinz Eugen' was ordered to the south-western corner of Serbia to attack Kraljevo, Ivanjica, Cacak, Kosovska Mitrovica, Uzice and Novi Pazar. The SS was supported by parts of the 9th Bulgarian Infantry Division.

On 5 October, SS-Obergruppenführer Artur Phleps, the commander of the 7th SS Division, ordered both German and Bulgarian forces to destroy the Chetnik forces. The German units assigned to crush the Chetniks were deployed in combat groups or *Kampfgruppen*: 'North' operating towards Zeljin, 'East' around Brus, 'South' in Gobella, and 'West' in the valley near Banje. Their strategy was to surround the partisans, block their escape, and then annihilate them. However, Chetnik corps were ordered to regroup into smaller squads, and with their superior knowledge of the area they were able to escape from the ring and disappear into the surrounding hills. Fighting was fierce with high casualty rates.

Unlike the Chetniks, the average SS soldier did not know the area he was fighting in, and was thus unaware of his immense task in crushing partisan activity. The soldiers were amazed by the immense forests, hills and mountains, and the many rivers and ravines that were continuously flooding. Also the little information they did have was often incorrect. Maps showed almost no roads, and when they did come across one, it was usually only a dirt track or in a terrible state of repair.

When the Chetniks escaped the ring, German and Bulgarian units took reprisals against the local population. In the village of Kriva Reka, 120 civilians were marched into the church and burned to death by members of the 7th SS Prinz Eugen. In the villages on Mount Goc 250 civilians were murdered. The village of Kopaonik (today a ski resort) saw the execution of around 300 civilians. On the march to the village, anyone found travelling on the road was hung or shot by the roadside.

The SS believed this would reduce partisan resistance, but it only incensed the Chetniks and made their opposition to the German regime even stronger.

Following this failure, SS Prinz Eugen undertook its next anti-partisan action, supported once again by Bulgarian forces. This time the operation was aimed along the Serbia–Montenegro border in the mountains east of the Ibar River. Again SS Prinz Eugen struggled in the mountains and hills and the operation was called off.

Undeterred, they mobilised another anti-partisan offensive in the Zagreb–Karlovac area, where German, Bulgarian and Italian forces attempted to defeat Partisans commanded by the notorious Josip Tito. Yet again, the operation failed due to the terrain and the Partisans managed to avoid any heavy fighting.

By the end of 1942, SS Prinz Eugen's military situation was stagnant. It had achieved some success in preventing or destroying partisan activity, but the area in which it was operating was too vast. Nonetheless, the New Year would bring further activity, as well as bloodshed to Tito's men and the Chetniks.

(**Above**) SS Prinz Eugen on the march with their pack animals. In the spring of 1942, the mountain division together with the Bulgarian Army were assigned to a large scale offensive aimed at clearing Chetnik forces in Serbia.

(**Opposite, above**) Here SS Prinz Eugen troops have marched into a Serbian village and removed the inhabitants from their buildings during an anti-partisan sweep. The local population paid a terrible price in reprisals for any partisan activity in their area. Civilians, men, women, young and old, were routinely seized and shot.

(**Opposite, below**) A column of motorcycle combinations advance along a dirt road through a Yugoslavian village. Note the Odal symbol of the Eugen Division painted in white on the front of the sidecar.

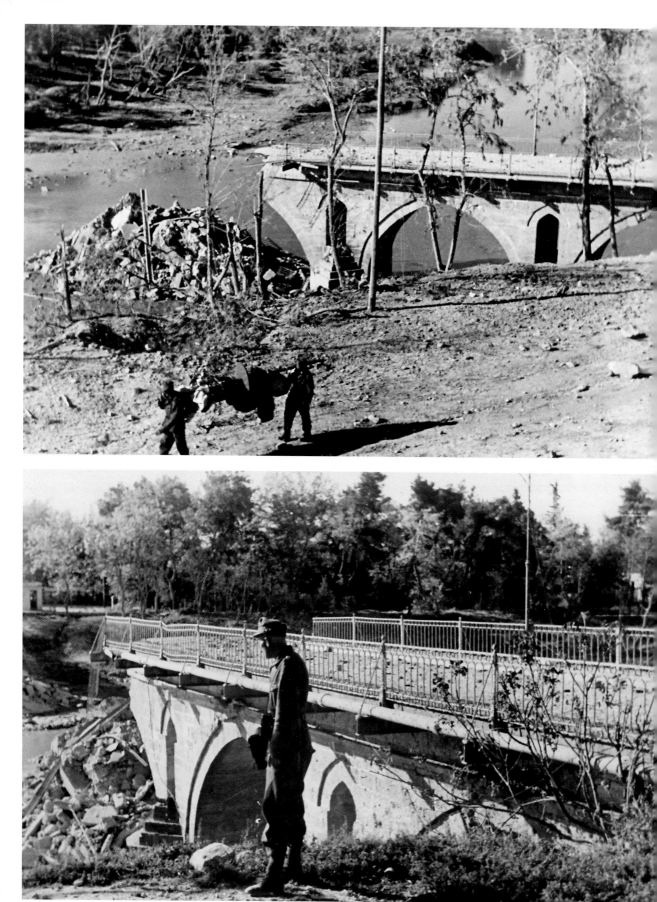

(**Opposite, above**) A bridge blown by a partisan demolition team. Note Gebirgs soldiers carrying supply bundles on a pole. Often units of the Gebirgsjäger supported SS Prinz Eugen in its operations in Yugoslavia.

(**Opposite, below**) The same bridge as in the previous photograph but this time showing a Gebirgs soldier surveying the damage. This soldier maybe attached to a mountain pioneer section. One of the jobs of a pioneer was to construct bridge sections and float them across a river.

(**Above**) A soldier walks through a Serbian town that has seen some extensive fighting. Partisans waged a brutal campaign in 1942 against the Germans across northern Serbia, attacking convoys, trains, rail links and roads. German and Bulgarian troops fought back, destroying towns and villages in the process, to terrorise and 'cleanse' the area. However, the partisans often withdrew into the surrounding hills, mountains and forests, making it considerably difficult to track them down.

Along a roadside a machine gun squad can be seen with their heavy 7.92mm MG34 on its Lafette 34 sustained-fire mount. The squad is relatively concealed and their uniforms blend in well with the local terrain. A light machine gun troop consisted of a gunner (No. 1), and two riflemen (Nos 2 and 3) to carry ammunition.

(**Opposite, above**) These SS troops conceal themselves well in a field during partisan operations. They wear the camouflage helmet cover as well as the camouflage smock first pattern. The smock was intended to be worn over the tunic, belt and equipment, with slash openings for easy access. However, it became widespread practice to wear the belt and equipment over the smock, making access easier.

(**Opposite, below**) Civilians often fled their towns if there was too much fighting in the area. Here civilians are seen with their carts full of possessions making their way to relative safety. Note Gebirgsjäger troops assisting the long column.

(**Opposite, above**) A flak gunner waves a national flag for aerial recognition during a Luftwaffe airstrike in the summer of 1942. Note the Sd.Kfz.10/4 halftrack mounting a 2cm flak gun. Tactical aerial bombardment served the German ground forces well, especially against positions difficult for troops to reach, but the lack of shelter was often problematic for the soldiers, especially in winter.

(**Opposite, below**) An interesting photograph showing a Bulgarian flak crew resting in the summer of 1942 with a German 8.8cm flak gun. Bulgarian forces supported the SS Prinz Eugen forces in Yugoslavia. It was in 1942 that the 1st Bulgarian Occupation Corps entered Serbia and immediately clashed with Partisan and Chetnik forces. The first large-scale anti-partisan action was by the 17th Infantry Division near the mountain of Pasiacha.

(**Above**) In the summer of 1942 and a camp has been erected by SS Prinz Eugen troops at the base of a hill using Zeltbahn shelter quarters. Foliage from the surrounding pine trees and other vegetation would have been used as bedding.

An interesting photograph showing a Bulgarian scouting mission supporting SS Prinz Eugen during an anti-partisan mission. The vehicle is a VW Type.82 Kfz.1 with Bulgarian markings.

What appears to be a forward artillery observation post and a Prinz Eugen observer estimates the range to a target using 6 × 30 Sf 14Z Scherenfernrohr (scissor binoculars). Observers scanned for weapon muzzles, moving infantry, armoured vehicles, fires, smoke from cooking and anything else they could detect to locate their enemy.

An SS Prinz Eugen column on a snowy road on the Serbia–Montenegro border in November 1942. SS troops can be seen on the march wearing the early white camouflage smock over what appears to be a standard army greatcoat. Note the vehicle with the Prinz Eugen insignia of the Odal rune painted on its right fender.

Troops clad in their winter whites are preparing to move out during a reconnaissance mission in late 1942. Many of the troops can be seen wearing the coloured friend-or-foe recognition stripes on both sleeves.

On a mountain road and a PaK crew can be seen. Most are wearing the single piece snow overall. Note the national flag draped on the road for aerial recognition.

An SS troop leader shouting orders to his men. He is wearing the Waffen-SS reversible parka grey side out and armed with an MP40. His kit comprises MP38/40 magazine pouches and 6 × 30 Zeiss binoculars.

In a trench, these SS soldiers are all clad in their winter whites, apart from one man. The extreme weather conditions in Yugoslavia coupled with the terrain made operations difficult. In the depths of winter 1942, partisan clearing almost stagnated due to the harsh weather.

An interesting photograph showing Gebirgs troops trying to move a staff vehicle that has become stuck on a snowy road. This picture was taken during operations supporting Bulgarian and Prinz Eugen forces along the Serbia–Montenegro border.

(**Above**) Along the Serbia–Montenegro border, a Gebirgsjäger MG34 machine gun squad can be seen positioned on a mountainside. All the troops wear the Zeltbahn. When the wearer didn't need it, it was usually rolled up and fitted to the personal equipment with two leather straps. The Zeltbahn was also sometimes attached to the D-rings of the Y-straps, or to the back of the leather belt.

(**Opposite**) A soldier is pictured here clad in his winter whites during a pause in a reconnaissance mission. Note he is wearing the special woollen toque beneath the *Bergmütze*. Typically troops wore two toques in the extreme arctic conditions. One was worn over the head to protect the ears and face, and one around the neck. They kept the head warm while wearing the steel helmet.

(**Above**) An MG34 machine gun squad advance through a wooded area to a new firing position. They wear the two-piece snow suit and M35 steel helmets, whitewashed for camouflage.

(**Opposite, above**) Though not widely implemented by SS Prinz Eugen, one of the quickest ways of moving from one part of the front to another was by ski. In this photograph a soldier, more than likely on a reconnaissance mission, is seen advancing across the snow with his backpack attached.

(**Opposite, below**) A ski patrol can be seen preparing to move. The two ski soldiers nearest the camera are wearing the shapeless two-piece snowsuit comprising a snow jacket and matching trousers. The jacket was buttoned all the way down the front with white painted buttons. It had a large white hood which could easily be pulled over the steel helmet. The hood helped conceal the headgear if it had not already received a winter covering, as well as affording protection to the back of the wearer's neck and ears.

Two photographs showing 6 × 30 Sf.14z Scherenfernrohr being used in the mountains of Yugoslavia. This is more than likely a Gebirgs artillery forward observation unit. A battery observation post often had two pairs of binoculars, one for engaging an enemy target and another for simultaneously searching and plotting additional enemy positions. Note the tripod-mounted binoculars being used on the slope. The observer can be seen adjusting the focus.

A group of soldiers pose for the camera. All are wearing the one-piece snowsuit. Stitched into their Bergmütze is the death head insignia of the Waffen-SS.

A whitewashed halftrack carrying troops clad in their discoloured winter reversibles. Although the winter reversible was a popular item of clothing it soon became dirty from constant wear, which rather defeated its camouflaging properties.

A machine gun squad use the surrounding pine trees as cover on the mountain slope. The light 7.92mm MG34 machine gun is on its bipod. The squad is relatively concealed, and their uniforms blend in well with the local terrain. Both soldiers are wearing improvised helmet covers to conceal their grey M1935 steel helmets.

Two soldier during a reconnaissance mission slowly negotiate a snowy mountain slope. Both men are wearing a fur-covered cap and the two-piece snow suit.

During a winter operation this flak crew are using their 2cm Flak gun against a ground target. Note the gunner's Flakvisier 35 sight and the way it is lined in elevation to the gun tube.

A ski-trooper wearing the two-piece snowsuit during operations in late 1942. He is armed with the standard army issue Karabiner 98K bolt action rifle, which has been whitewashed.

Ski troops using a sled to move from one part of the front to another. Wheeled transport was often useless in the trackless wastes and forests of Yugoslavia.

Chapter Three

1943 – Operation Weiss

By early 1943 the situation on the Eastern Front was becoming a worry for German commanders, and the Axis situation in North Africa had also deteriorated. German high command was concerned about the possibility of an Allied landing in the Balkans and that resistance forces in Yugoslavia, such as the Chetniks and Tito's Partisans, would interfere and hamper German defensive operations. With this in mind, Hitler ordered the Armed Forces Commander in south-east Europe, General Alexander Lohr, to commence widespread anti-partisan actions and destroy the resistance in Yugoslavia. On 8 January 1943, Lohr and Mario Roatta, commanders of the 2nd Italian Army, met in Zagreb to discuss a plan to crush partisan resistance.

A large-scale operation was planned to be carried out in three stages; it was named Operation Weiss. The third stage was cancelled, but the first stage, Weiss 1, was aimed at the destruction of the Partisans of Banija, Cazinska, Grmec, Lika and Grmec. Weiss 2 was aimed at Partisan activities in the south-east and covered the areas of Bihac Republic, Drvar, Glamoc, Jaice and Kljuc.

Some 90,000 German, Bulgarian and Italian troops and twelve air squadrons were ordered to destroy the central command of the Partisan movement quickly and decisively. German High Command sent out an order to be ruthless in the treatment of all captured Partisans and the civilian population. Everyone would be deemed to be hostile, all Partisans captured would be executed, and the civilian population deported to transit camps. All villages in the combat area were to be razed to the ground, and commanders in the field were forbidden from punishing their subordinates for severity.

For the first phase of the operation, Weiss 1, four German divisions were assembled: 7th SS Prinz Eugen, and 369th, 714th and 717th divisions. They were to attack alongside three Italian divisions on the right wing advancing through Lika and northern Dalmatia. Their objective was to encircle and destroy the Partisans and to deport the local population.

The partisans were as determined as ever to continue resisting, sabotaging and killing their enemy. Although guerrilla operations would never win the war, the strategy was to stem the tide and delay the advancing enemy long enough to allow for a favorable political settlement.

Weiss 1 was mobilised on 20 January 1943. Partisan activity was strong and fanatical, but slowly the line, which had withstood a number of heavy attacks, cracked and was pushed back. Sunj was captured on 24 January, and three days later Rakovica fell. Bihac was entered on 29 January without a fight. The 7th SS Prinz Eugen continued its drive towards Petrovac against a string of Partisan defences, mainly the 7th Banija. The Partisans tried their best to avoid pitched battles, preferring little-by-little to weaken the advancing German troops and thus make them easy prey. On 7 February, 7th SS Prinz Eugen reached Petrovac and two days later managed to line up with the 717th Division. The 369th then joined the SS near Bihac.

The second phase of the operation, Weiss 2, commenced on 25 February with a concentric attack on Livno. It was planned that the Partisans would be pushed back, encircled and annihilated there. Two divisions were used: 7th SS Prinz Eugen and the 369th. The route assigned to the SS was from Bosanski Petrovac, over Drvar and Bosansko Grahovo to Livno. The 369th was ordered to cover the route from Mrkonjić Grad. In front of them stood six brigades of the Partisan 1st Bosnian Corps. Although the Partisans knew they were no match against their Waffen-SS foe, they planned to resist long enough to allow its own units and population to be evacuated.

Over the next few days the 7th SS Prinz Eugen pushed forward, capturing Drvar on 28 February. It then battled on towards Grahovo, capturing the town in early March. Partisan forces, though mauled and weakened by the Waffen-SS attacks, withdrew and dispersed into the mountains with refugees, marching over the Šator Mountain towards Tore and then back to the Krajina. The 7th SS Prinz Eugen pursued the Partisans, but over the coming weeks and months were unable to take any effective action against them due to the rugged terrain.

On 10 July 1943 an Allied invasion overwhelmed the defending German and Italian forces on Sicily, and on 3 September the British Eighth Army landed on the toe of Italy, the day the Italian government agreed to an armistice with the Allies.

As a result of the Allied invasion of Italy, the 7th SS Prinz Eugen became part of the XV Mountain Corps and was transferred to operations along the Dalmatian coast. Operation Axis was mounted to round up the last remnants of the Italian army there and impose German control in the area.

On 22 October 1943, following Operation Axis, the division was renamed the 7th SS Volunteer Mountain Division Prinz Eugen. It was then thrown into another operation, Lightning Ball, and then another weeks later in December, Operation Waldrausch. During these operations a number of missions were carried out in freezing driving rain and snow-storms. Due to the miserable conditions there was a high incidence of trench foot, which had a bad effect on the morale of the men. In turn, the area the SS had seized could not be controlled properly and partisan activity escalated. The operation however was not abandoned: the SS mountain troops were determined to destroy partisan activity in the area.

This photograph, taken in the early winter of 1943, shows a commanding officer with his men before Operation Weiss. The first stage of Weiss, called 'Weiss 1', was aimed at the destruction of Partisan-held areas of Banija, Cazinska, Grmec, Lika and Grmec.

A supply cart crosses one of the many wooden bridges that spanned the rivers of Banija, Cazinska, Grmec, Lika and Grmec. Note troops behind the wagon dressed in single white camouflage sheets and armed with the Karabiner 98K bolt action rifle slung over their shoulders.

(**Above**) During the Weiss cleansing operation troops are seen with an early variant whitewashed Sturmgeschütz III which is protecting their column against possible enemy attacks along a snowy road. Note the injured soldier on the right with his left eye bandaged.

(**Opposite, above**) An interesting photograph taken from the cupola of a Sturmgeschütz III showing regular and SS Prinz Eugen troops covering a hole in a road with wood to allow their column to continue its drive.

(**Opposite, below**) A crew during a pause in action rest next to their 7.5cm PaK 40. This weapon was considered the workhorse of the infantry and anti-tank units.

Here Prinz Eugen troops can be seen following a mountain road during operations in the early spring of 1943. Transporting equipment to the front across rugged and mountainous terrain was usually undertaken by pack mules. These hardy creatures were well suited for rough terrain and were used extensively throughout the war.

A soldier who has just climbed a mountainside pauses during his march. He wears the summer camouflage smock and is armed with a 7.9mm Kar 98k carbine. This Mauser was the standard shoulder arm for both the Wehrmacht and the Waffen-SS. (NARA)

A photograph of a SS-Obersturmführer during spring operations in 1943. He wears a Waffen-SS camouflage smock with a pair of 6 × 30 Zeiss binoculars around his neck. Attached to his black leather belt are 32-round ammunition pouches for his 9mm MP40 machine pistol.

On patrol on a mountain mission. Both soldiers wear the standard issue Gebirgs rucksack, which appears to be heavily laden with supplies.

A column of Prinz Eugen Division motorcycles with their sidecar combinations advance through a village. Motorcycles such as the famous BMW R75 or the Zündapp KS750 were intended for traditional cavalry missions of reconnaissance and screening. They scouted ahead and to the flanks of advancing units to assess enemy location, strength and intention. Their primary role was reconnaissance, but they would engage light targets and at times attempt to capture enemy patrols. Note the SS Prinz Eugen insignia painted on the front of the leading sidecar. (NARA)

A forward observation post during operations in the spring of 1943. Two radiomen can be seen communicating to one of the many field posts scattered in the rear. *(NARA)*

SS Prinz Eugen troops pose for the camera during a pause in operations in the spring of 1943. Three are ranked SS-Unterscharführer and wear the familiar death head badges associated with the Waffen-SS. *(NARA)*

Inside a position in a mountainside and a radioman can be seen with a Tornisterfunkgerät b1 (Torn.Fu.b1) (S/E) or 'pack radio'. These sets were widely used by both the Wehrmacht and Waffen-SS and were carried in two parts by the radiomen on specially designed back-pack frames. This is obviously a forward observation post and one of the soldiers can be seen with a clipboard for collating information. *(NARA)*

A typical position during operations in Yugoslavia. Here Prinz Eugen soldiers have set up a camp using their Zeltbahn shelter as a tent to protect themselves from the wind and driving rain. *(NARA)*

A mortar crew negotiates undergrowth during an operation in the summer of 1943. The leading soldier carries the gun tube in a case; the man behind him carries an ammunition box; and the soldier behind him has it attached to the Y-straps on his back. *(NARA)*

A group of Prinz Eugen soldiers in the summer of 1943. During this period the 7th SS were operating in the Šator Mountain around Tore and Krajina. The troops pursued bands of partisans, but the terrain favoured the defenders and they were unable to take any effective action against them.

The crew of a 15cm sIG33 infantry gun pose for the camera. These guns, operated by specially trained infantrymen, were regarded as workhorse pieces.

A 3.7cm PaK35/36 gun crew during a partisan operation in the summer of 1943. Although by mid-war this gun was outdated, it had its advantages: it could be brought up to a position by as few as two men; being small it was easy to conceal; and it had a good rate of fire. (NARA)

Two photographs taken in sequence showing a forward observation post during the late summer of 1943. Signalmen can be seen operating a portable radio. This device was the standard radio used at battalion and regimental level. When carried on their back-pack frame they could be connected to each other (upper and lower valves) via special cables and used on the march, as in this photograph. (NARA)

Chapter Four

Guerilla Warfare

The new year of 1944 was one of major decisions for the German army on both the Italian and eastern fronts. In Russia, the situation was as dire as ever with all fronts more or less on the retreat or cracking under the strain of constant Soviet attacks. On the Italian front the Allies were slowly making progress across rugged terrain and strong defensive lines.

SS Prinz Eugen received a new commander, SS-Oberführer Otto Kumm, who was aware of the division's reputation for steadiness in action. He also knew that it had performed well in mountain warfare but had had a hard time against the Yugoslav partisans. He needed to give his men renewed determination, vigor and confidence.

But psychology was not enough. They had neither enough weapons or troops for their new operation, Waldrausch. The partisans were well-armed, often equipped with captured German fighting vehicles.

Another problem the SS faced was the trench systems, which had been constructed by the partisans. From these trenches they would attack an enemy column or position, then withdraw back into their own trenches where they could survive for many days.

Time and time again German forces carried out offensives to clear certain areas, and at the end of a sweep they found the partisans would come back again. This had been the pattern of the Prinz Eugen Division's life. It fought hard, sometimes in extreme weather conditions, to clear out a guerrilla force, often having to clear out the same area again only a few weeks later.

With the support of the Allies, supplies for the partisans, brought in by air drops, became abundant, and the balance of power began to swing in favor of the partisans. But SS Prinz Eugen was still determined to crush guerilla activity wherever they could find it, and fighting continued to rage with losses on both sides.

Kumm could see that the partisans were now stronger than ever. In spite of orders to crush them, it was clear that his division could only contain them. He carried out patrols aggressively and without high expenditure of ammunition.

Eventually the Germans realised that Tito was such a powerful and valuable asset to the partisans that they decided to launch an operation to capture or kill him. Operation Rosselsprung began on 25 May 1944. It was spearheaded by the

500th SS Fallschirmjäger-Bataillon supported by the Brandenburg Regiment. Two companies of the 500th were dropped directly on Tito's supposed headquarters while the other two were landed by glider. However, Tito evaded capture, and by the time the Germans arrived in the cave where the partisan leader had been hiding, he had already boarded a train and taken himself to safety. The operation had failed miserably and in the process the Germans had fought against superior Yugoslav partisans who had driven off, killed or wounded most of the SS paratroopers.

The Germans then moved to destroy Tito's finest fighting formation, the 1st Proletarian Division. Initially the operation showed signs of success with some of the Proletarian crack units being badly mauled by SS Prinz Eugen. However, most of the Proletarian Division evaded destruction and escaped eastwards into Serbia.

By the first week of August 1944 operations came to an end, with Tito's forces still withdrawing eastwards through the hills and mountain ranges of Serbia. But the situation for the German army in the Balkans was more precarious than it had ever been. With Bulgaria declaring war on Germany, and Romania signing an armistice with the Soviet Union, German withdrawal from the Balkans became inevitable.

The Bulgarians wasted no time moving its Fifth Army to the rear of German Army Group E, while the Thrace Bulgarian Division threatened its flanks. The Germans knew they could deal with the Bulgarians, but their biggest threat was the advance of Soviet forces in support. To prevent a collapse of the German army's southern flank the Supreme Commander South planned an operation to attack enemy forces escaping into Serbia. This operation was known as Rubezahl.

(**Right**) A portrait photograph of SS-Oberführer Otto Kumm who took command of the Prinz Eugen Division on 30 January 1944. In this photograph Kumm is ranked as an SS-Standartenführer. As an officer he had earned his reputation on the battlefield as the commander of the Der Führer Regiment of the SS Das Reich Division from July 1941 to April 1943.

(**Opposite**) Two photographs showing a column of Gebirgstruppen on the march along a snowy mountain road in the early winter of 1944. These soldiers are supporting the Prinz Eugen division along with Bulgarian forces in a desperate attempt to suppress Tito's partisans.

Prinz Eugen troops tuck into their rations during a pause in operations in March 1944. In January of that year the 7th SS had been transferred to the Split and Dubrovnik areas for refit, training and reorganisation. *(NARA)*

Nine photographs showing a rare glimpse at Bulgarian armoured forces. This armoured support was used with the Prinz Eugen Division in its anti-partisan actions of mid-1944. In March 1944 the Bulgarian army acquired a number of German armoured vehicles including some 97 Pz.Kpfw.IVs, Ausf G and H variants. They were designated as Maybach T-IV. They also obtained the Sturmgeschütz III, known in Bulgaria as the Maybach T-III. Some of the photographs show the usual markings of the Bulgarian army including the typical styling of the vehicle registrations plates. By August 1944 the Bulgarian army had turned these armoured vehicles against Germany and fought alongside the Soviets.

A soldier wrapped in a Zeltbahn lies in front of a pill box that appears to have received considerable action with pockmarks around the opening.

Prinz Eugen soldiers interrogate two locals on a mountainside during anti-partisan sweeps in the spring of 1944. By this time partisan operations were continuing aggressively even though the political position was changing. The Soviet army were advancing towards the Balkans and the Bulgarian army were poised to declare war on Germany, which would completely change the situation in Yugoslavia and force Prinz Eugen to withdraw from the area.

Gebirgs troops on a foot march along a mountain road in the summer of 1944. The Gebirgs and Prinz Eugen troops had to march long distances on roads which were always hazardous due to partisan activity.

A Prinz Eugen tank unit with captured French Hotchkiss H38 tanks halted along a mountain road. Following the victory over the French in 1940 the German army acquired a considerable amount of captured armour and distributed it across its units. The Hotchkiss was a sturdy reliable vehicle and was used throughout operations by the 7th SS in Yugoslavia. (NARA)

Prinz Eugen troops salute the fallen at a graveside in the summer of 1944. (NARA)

Two photographs showing Prinz Eugen troops resting following what was probably an arduous march. Both photographs shows the soldiers with their 98K carbines at close hand. In the second image the soldiers is sleeping on his kit. Note the rifle ammunition pouches for his Mauser attached to his black leather belt. He is wearing the distinctive summer camouflage smock of the Waffen-SS. (NARA)

Prinz Eugen troops negotiate one of the many streams in the mountain ranges in Yugoslavia in the summer of 1944. (NARA)

Two SS-Standartenführer converse on the edge of a Yugoslav village during guerrilla operations in the summer of 1944. By the first week of August 1944, partisan operations came to an end with Tito's forces retreating through the hills. (NARA)

Prinz Eugen troops pause and during their rest period are seen cleaning and preparing their weapons. This time was often known by soldiers as 'clean and patch hour'. (*NARA*)

Out in the mountains, an opportunity to see a PaK crew with their 3.7cm PaK35/36 anti-tank gun during an operation in mid-1944. While this gun was now regarded as outmoded, it still undertook sterling service against lighter enemy forces. (*NARA*)

Two soldiers look down at a horse which is either injured, sick or possibly dead. The mountain terrain put a heavy strain on these animals. They often had to carry a considerable quantity of equipment. Troops needed several days rations, cold weather clothing, climbing equipment, as well as arms and ammunition. *(NARA)*

Front line troops surveying the terrain ahead through their 6 × 30 Zeiss binoculars. They all wear the summer camouflage smocks of the Waffen-SS and are mainly armed with the Karabiner 98K bolt action rifle. *(NARA)*

Two SS troopers negotiating a mountain range during a summer operation. The soldier nearest to the camera has full camouflage attire, the SS helmet cover and the camouflage smock. He wears the standard issue equipment supplied to an SS mountain soldier. He has a full set of kit including an M1938 gasmask in its metal canister, entrenching tool, M1931 field flask and S84/98 bayonet for his Karabiner 98K rifle. He also wears the mountain rucksack. The soldier is handing his comrade weapons, which have been bound together. (*NARA*)

A Prinz Eugen Panzertruppe wearing the special black Panzer uniform with M1938 black cap and death head badge. The uniform was the same design and colouring for all ranks of the Panzer arm including generals. The collar patch has the insignia of the Prinz Eugen Division. (*NARA*)

(**Opposite, above**) Heavily laden front-line Prinz Eugen troops during a summer operation along the Serbian border in 1944, more than likely undertaking a reconnaissance mission. This patrol can obviously see a great distance, but in the mountains the enemy could at any time be round the next corner or behind the next tree. (*NARA*)

(**Opposite, below**) A captured shelter used by SS troops. Although such shelters did not provide much in the way of protection against heavy enemy fire, they did provide adequate shelter against the bitter mountain elements.

Two commanders in the field consider some information during an operation in 1944. The man on the left is an SS Standartenführer. (*NARA*)

During an anti-partisan operation these Prinz Eugen troops are conferring before resuming their march. The commander nearest in the picture is wearing his familiar Waffen-SS camouflage smock and field cap. *(NARA)*

A young Prinz Eugen soldier poses for the camera with a group of his comrades. The trooper wears the summer camouflage smock and the distinctive Waffen-SS field service cap or Feldmütze. The death head emblem is stitched on the front of his cap. (NARA)

An 8.8cm FlaK crew prepare their weapon for action. During the war many of the 8.8cm FlaK guns were fitted with shields making them dual-purpose anti-aircraft and anti-tank guns. Some were even modified for bunker-busting and anti-tank roles, while others were mounted on semi-armoured half-tracks.

Bulgarian troops advancing towards the ridge of Strazhin in Macedonia in October 1944. With Bulgaria now at war against Germany and its allies, it fought in Macedonia to the old borders of Bulgaria while the Russians advanced towards the area bringing increasing pressure on the German forces to withdraw.

MG42 crews negotiating the mountain ranges during partisan operations in August 1944.

Chapter Five

Last Months

Operation Rubezahl was chiefly fought by the 1st Gebirgsjäger Division and SS Prinz Eugen's 14th Regiment but was supported during its initial phase by the 13th 'Handschar' and 21st 'Skanderbeg' SS Gebirgs divisions. At first Rubezahl went well with the mountain troops, hitting the partisans hard, encircling and subduing them. However, as before, many of the partisans escaped to fight again. Undeterred, on 22 August 1944 a combined operation by the 1st Gebirgs and Prinz Eugen divisions encircled one large partisan force. Fighting was fierce, and slowly the partisans trapped inside the pocket were ground down against numerically superior forces. They were eventually destroyed, but not before many of the wounded were fortunate enough to be flown out of the pocket to safety and shipped to hospitals in Italy by US and British forces.

SS Prinz Eugen were then tasked to prevent the partisans reaching Belgrade. Kumm was aware that his division were overstretched and would not be able disperse enemy formations. However, just days into the action, he was ordered to withdraw from the battle and march his men to take over the 1st Gebirgs Division's positions around Nish. Kumm's men had effectively been deployed in a 'fire brigade' role. The premier Waffen-SS units were often used in this role, being shuttled from one danger spot to another to get others out of trouble. It was now down to the men of SS Prinz Eugen to demonstrate how effective they could be as a special fire brigade force. The division was ordered to the Danube to confront advancing Red Army forces for the first time. The Soviets had already established bridgeheads on its banks. Kumm had not only to contain the Russian forces from breaking out, but also to hold back Bulgarian troops advancing from the east and the south, whilst simultaneously fighting partisan forces. All this had to be achieved until Army Group E, now withdrawing from Greece, had marched through Nish. Fighting to hold Nish would prove to be the fiercest and hardest battle that SS Prinz Eugen had ever fought. Although regarded as a second-rate SS division these troops were formidable opponents, but despite their best efforts nothing could mask the fact that they were dwarfed by the superiority of the Red Army. They were isolated with hardly any support and holding a line nearly 100 miles long surrounding by woods infested with guerrillas. Kumm had no choice but to hold the line. On the left his men faced the

57th Red Army, which had advanced across the Serbian border and was marching at speed towards Zajecar. On the right they faced the 2nd Bulgarian Army, which had now entered Nish and was fighting against overstretched Prinz Eugen units. Within days both Zajecar and Nish had erupted into urban warfare. By the end of October 1944, SS Prinz Eugen reported it only had 3,460 of all ranks fit for duty. On the 29th Kumm reported, 'As a result of the past months defensive fighting in the Nish area against an enemy in overwhelming strength the division has suffered heavy losses in men and equipment. The greatest number of its vehicles and heavy weapons as well as the majority of its horses have been lost. Division is, therefore, compelled to rely upon unreliable reinforcements for its artillery and signals. Particularly serious is the lack of anti-tank guns. Only in a few isolated cases could the enemy's numerical superiority affect the fighting spirit of our troops. The great mass of the division remained unshaken. In fact the combat efficiency of the units is higher now than at the beginning of the heavy fighting and this is due to the success that the division has achieved both in offensive as well as in defensive battles.'

The division fought on to keep the main road open for Army Group E to move westwards to Sarajevo. The defence continued until the end of November when reports confirmed that the Russians had decided to withdraw from the area after failing to make a successful breakthrough. The Soviet formations were moved to other sectors of the Balkans and they were replaced with Bulgarian units and partisans.

Against the Bulgarians and partisans Prinz Eugen defended more successfully and caused considerable losses to their enemy. In the days running up to the new year the division was still protecting Army Group E as it headed towards the River Save.

The year of 1945 opened with a large-scale Russian offensive to cut lines of communication including the important rail link. Along the whole front Russian artillery supported reconnaissance attacks and pulverised German positions. The Red Army air force also conducted numerous sorties.

The Russian offensive had ripped open a gap in the German lines. The front needed to be closed before it collapsed altogether. It was SS Prinz Eugen that bore the brunt of this and relieved the pressure on the 2nd Panzer Army which was fighting for its life on the north bank of the Danube. The counter-offensive, codenamed Spring Storm, opened on 17 January. A few days later, Kumm left to take command of the premier 1st SS Panzer Division 'Leibstandarte'. His replacement was Brigadeführer August Schmidhuber, who had initially commanded the SS Freiwilligen Gebirgsjäger Regiment 14 'Skanderbeg' of the 7th SS. He was then promoted to SS Standartenführer when he commanded the 21st Waffen Mountain Division of the SS 'Skanderbeg' (1st Albanian). In June 1944 he was promoted to SS Oberführer and then to Brigadeführer when he took command of SS Prinz Eugen.

A new German offensive, codenamed 'Wehrwolf', opened on 4 February, and SS Prinz Eugen took part 'with energy and fortitude' serving in the LXXXXI Corps. The operation was not very successful and lasted about three weeks.

In the last week of February SS Prinz Eugen was transferred to Army Group reserve where it fought as an emergency 'fire brigade' in the Zenica area. Zenica was a strategically important town north of Sarajevo. Already partisan forces had begun encircling German units, and if they succeeded they would cut the retreat line for all the German forces in the south of Yugoslavia. SS Prinz Eugen was committed to open the pathway for the withdrawal and keep the key roads and rail lines open. The 7th SS Prinz Eugen fought with skill and tenacity, driving the partisans away from the town and restoring the area.

With Zenica captured the division was ordered to scale the Igman Mountain and go on to capture the Treskavia Panina. The operation was difficult with deep snow, driving winds and freezing temperatures. Men and animals struggled with their packs carrying supplies and heavy weapons. In spite of the conditions and unfavourable terrain, SS units managed to drive partisan forces out of the mountains, at least temporarily. Yugoslavian troops soon stormed the mountain in a counter-attack supported by partisans. Fighting raged for several weeks and losses were high, but eventually SS Prinz Eugen drove Yugoslav forces to the lower slopes in a series of bitter clashes.

In mid-April around the town of Zenica the rearguard of the SS division were ordered to hold the main westward road open to allow the XXI Gebirgsjäger Corps to pass through and withdraw. Once the mountain corps had successfully passed through, an order was issued to SS Prinz Eugen to start its own withdrawal north-wards out of Bosnia through Croatia and into southern Austria. The withdrawal was swift and hampered only by the Sava River where the whole division had to cross with assault boats due to the main bridges being blown by partisans. The division continued its march up the Belgrade–Zagreb highway. As it withdrew it came across many abandoned vehicles and heavy weapons that Army Group E had left as it too retreated northwards through Yugoslavia towards the Austrian border. Partisan and Yugoslav forces were determined to hinder the withdrawal and SS Prinz Eugen was forced to engage in further battles along the way.

During the last week of April 1945, when the Reich was in the grip of defeat, the 7th SS Prinz Eugen fought a series of battles west of Zagreb to allow encircled German forces to escape. On 2 May, when Italian forces surrendered, the 7th SS sent its 13th Regiment to positions south of Karlovac.

Over the next few days they tried desperately to hold a position around Karlovac, but finally SS Prinz Eugen was forced to march again towards Austria. During the evening of 8 May an order was sent out to all units that a general capitulation was to come into effect the following day. This order spurred the SS on to reach Austria as quickly as possible, fearing for their lives if they fell into the hands of the partisans. The SS were aware that the partisan forces would not hesitate to violate any armistice agreement, and sent out orders to its units that they were to retaliate if fired upon.

With the war ended the 7th SS continued its withdrawal through Yugoslavia. All the roads northwards were blocked by Army Group E's columns of vehicles and carts, as they desperately tried to escape into Austria. However, by 11 May many of them were captured and were forced to lay down their arms, and five days later the remnants of the 7th Waffen SS Gebirgsjäger Division Prinz Eugen finally surrendered to the Yugoslavs. The SS had committed appalling atrocities against many innocent Yugoslav civilians and as these soldiers were disarmed little mercy was shown on them. Few returned to their families or loved ones.

(**Below**) A road march during the summer of 1944. The pack animals are well laden with equipment and a number of them can be seen attached with carriers, which were commonly used by mountain troops to carry their rations and other supplies. (*NARA*)

(**Opposite, above**) Here SS troops can be seen with their pack animals. Mules or horses were SS Prinz Eugen's main means of transporting equipment to the front across rugged terrain. Note the basket carriers that were attached to the horses to carry supplies. (*NARA*)

(**Opposite, below**) Two Prinz Eugen soldiers out in the field both wearing the summer camouflage smock and field cap. (*NARA*)

During a pause in a partisan sweep, Prinz Eugen troops can be seen with prisoners. In August 1944, the partisan operation continued with unabated ferocity and Prinz Eugen were tasked with trying to prevent the partisans from reaching Belgrade. *(NARA)*

Here a soldier collects firewood while two of his comrades are seen with a piece of sheeting, obviously for some kind of warmth on the mountainside. During the winter, soldiers needed all the warmth and shelter they could get. *(NARA)*

A weary infantryman rests on a mountainside and sleeps under his Zeltbahn. His comrades either side have covered themselves completely with sheeting to keep warm. Note all their kit including steel helmet with SS decal printed on the side. Straw for the horses has been strewn on the ground for the comfort and warmth of the men. (NARA)

A heavily laden pack animal during operations in 1944. (NARA)

(**Above**) Wearing their distinctive winter whites during a partisan operation these mortar troops are about to fire their 8cm Granatwerfer 34 (8cm GrW34), which was the standard German infantry mortar used throughout the war.

(**Opposite, above**) An SS soldier is wearing his reversible fur lined winter anorak while watching a smouldering T-34 Soviet tank in January 1945. The 7th SS fought partisans near Otok, and later were sent to the Vukovar area where they fought against advancing Soviet forces and Tito's partisans.

(**Opposite, below**) An SS trooper makes his way through wreckage following bitter fighting against Soviet forces in January 1945. Behind the soldier is a knocked-out T-34.

Two SS soldiers clad in winter whites during the late war period. The trooper on the left is drinking from his canteen. He is armed with the 7.9mm StG 44 assault rifle and carries two three-pocket pouches holding 30-round magazines.

(**Opposite, above**) A group of Yugoslav partisans have been captured and sit in a field waiting for a fate that can only be imagined. Thousands of men and women were caught by the 7th SS and its allies between 1943 and 1945 and were indiscriminately put to death by firing squads.

(**Opposite, below**) A group of front line Prinz Eugen troops are seen on a mountainside. Two squad leaders are taking notes, probably during a reconnaissance mission. They all wear the summer camouflage smocks. (*NARA*)

Two photographs taken in sequence showing an artillery crew preparing to fire their 7.5cm Feldkanone 16 neuer Art (7.5cm FK.16.nA) artillery piece. This weapon dated back to the First World War. It was originally intended as a horse-drawn cavalry-accompanying gun, but eventually found itself with any type of German formation that was in need of a light gun and was frequently used with motorised traction. The Gebirgsjäger, the Waffen-SS Nord and 7th SS Prinz Eugen were often seen with these old weapons in their units until to the end of the war. (NARA)

During an enemy contact these Prinz Eugen mortar troops can be seen with an 8cm Gr.W34 mortar. During the war the mortar had become the standard infantry support weapon giving the soldier valuable high explosive capability beyond the range of riles or hand grenades. It was particularly effective for use in mountains. One of the major drawbacks was its inaccuracy: even an experienced mortar crew generally required ten bombs to achieve a direct hit on a target. (*NARA*)

(**Opposite**) Two photographs showing a Prinz Eugen machine gunner with his MG37. This gun was originally known as the ZB-37 and mass produced in Czechoslovakia for the Czech military, but once they fell under German control they were renamed. Only 6,400 of these weapons were issued to Waffen-SS and Polizei units. They were either mounted on tanks or armoured vehicles, or ground mounted. (*NARA*)

(**Above**) Two photographs showing Prinz Eugen troops preparing food on a mountainside during a pause in their march. The troops were well trained in survival and usually had plenty of provisions to sustain them. Often the soldiers marched for days without coming across any villages or towns. It was imperative that each man knew how to survive in the most inhospitable places. (*NARA*)

A Prinz Eugen unit on a mountainside. The soldiers' uniforms blend well with the surrounding vegetation and local terrain. Although their equipment was much the same as for other infantrymen, there were differences. The mountain troopers were provided with larger water bottles and special high-capacity rucksacks. They had heavy, sturdy climbing boots and puttees, wind jackets, snow camouflage suits, and other cold weather clothing. Specially trained troops also received ice-axes, hard-lay climbing rope, pitons and piton hammers, carabiners, as well as avalanche marker cords and searching flags. *(NARA)*

During operations in the mountains this SS soldier can be seen moving stealthily around the rocks armed with his Mauser 7.9mm Kar98k carbine. *(NARA)*

A Prinz Eugen patrol during a mountain climbing expedition, more than likely a posed shot. These soldiers wear the camouflage helmet cover as well as the camouflage smock. The smock has the predominantly brown, autumn, camouflage patterns outermost. Note the full mountain kit the soldier is wearing on the right. (*NARA*)

A flamethrower soldier being prepared for an action against an enemy position. The flamethrower comprised a small cylinder that contained compressed nitrogen propellant. The weapon was usually fired in two to three second bursts and was operated by a trigger that simultaneously released the fuel stream and ignited. The flamethrower was particularly useful for destroying the enemy positioned inside bunkers, trenches, caves, and other areas where it was difficult to achieve results with firing weapons or shells.

A group of Prinz Eugen troops clad in their camouflage smocks and their M43 field caps with Waffen-SS machine woven cap insignia. On the left flap, though not seen in this photograph, the cap normally displayed the machine-embroidered Edelweiss insignia of the SS mountain units. One of the soldiers, ranked as a Schütze, wears the Odal rune emblem, though blurred, of the 7th SS division. *(NARA)*

A photograph taken during the last weeks of the war showing various support vehicles and a column of SS and Wehrmacht troops on a road withdrawing from the Balkans. On the road is a stationary Jagdpanzer IV. In front of the panzer is a Volkswagen Schwimmwagen with officers being chauffeured to the rear.

Order of Battle & Commanders

Order of Battle: December 1942

SS Gebirgsjäger Regiment 1
– 3 × Gebirgsjäger Battaillon
SS Gebirgsjäger Regiment 2
– 3 × Gebirgsjäger Battaillon
SS Freiwilligen Gebirgs Artillerie Regiment
– Abteilungen 1 to 4
SS Freiwilligen Gebirgs Aufklärungs Abteilung
SS Kradschütz Battaillon
SS Panzer Abteilung
SS Panzerjäger Abteilung

SS Gebirgs Pionier Battaillon
SS Gebirgs Flak Abteilung
SS Radfahr Battaillon
SS Kavallerie Abteilung
SS Gebirgs Nachrichten Abteilung
SS Gebirgs Feldersatz Battaillon
SS Sanitäts Abteilung
SS Feldgendarmerie Trupp 7
SS Freiwilligen Gebirgs Veterinär Kompanie 7
SS Divisions Versorgungs Truppen

Order of Battle: 22 October 1943

SS Freiwilligen Gebirgsjäger Regiment 13
   'Artur Phleps'
– 3 × Gebirgsjäger Battaillon
SS Freiwilligen Gebirgsjäger Regiment 14
   'Skanderberg'
– 3 × Gebirgsjäger Battaillon
SS Freiwilligen Gebirgs Artillerie Regiment 7
– Abteilungen 1 to 4
SS Freiwilligen Gebirgs Aufklärungs
   Abteilung (mot) 7
SS Panzer Abteilung 7
SS Panzerjäger Abteilung 7

SS Gebirgs Pionier Battaillon 7
SS Gebirgs Flak Abteilung 7
SS Radfahr Battaillon 7
SS Kavallerie Abteilung 7
SS Gebirgs Nachrichten Abteilung 7
SS Gebirgs Feldersatz Battaillon 7
SS Sanitäts Abteilung 7
SS Feldgendarmerie Trupp 7
SS Freiwilligen Gebirgs Veterinär Kompanie 7
SS Freiwilligen Gebirgs Kriegsberichter Zug 7
SS Divisions Versorgungs Truppen 7

Order of Battle: 1944

SS Freiwilligen Gebirgsjäger Regiment 13
   'Artur Phleps'
– 3 × Gebirgsjäger Battaillon
SS Freiwilligen Gebirgsjäger Regiment 14
   'Skanderbeg'

– 3 × Gebirgsjäger Battaillon
SS Freiwilligen Gebirgs Artillerie Regiment 7
– Abteilungen 1 to 4
SS Freiwilligen Gebirgs Aufklärungs
   Abteilung (mot) 7

SS Panzer Abteilung 7

SS Panzer Aufklärungs Zug

SS Gebirgs Panzerjäger Abteilung 7

SS Sturmgeschütz Abteilung 7

SS Gebirgs Pionier Battaillon 7

SS Flak Abteilung 7

SS Radfahr Aufklärungs Abteilung 7

SS Kavallerie Abteilung 7

SS Kradschützen Battalion 7

SS Gebirgs Nachrichten Abteilung 7

SS Feldersatz Abteilung 7

SS Sanitäts Abteilung 7

SS Freiwilligen Gebirgs Veterinär Kompanie 7

SS Freiwilligen Gebirgs Kriegsberichter Zug 7

SS Propaganda Zug

SS Feldgendarmerie Trupp 7

SS Werkstatt Kompanie

SS Nachschub Kompanie 7

SS Instandsetzung Abteilung 7

SS Wirtschafts Battaillon 7

SS Wehrgeologisches Battaillon

Commanders

SS Obergruppenführer Artur Phleps	(January 1942 – May 1943)
SS Brigadeführer Carl Reichsritter von Oberkamp	(May 1943 – January 1944)
SS Brigadeführer Otto Kumm	(January 1944 – 20 January 1945)
SS Brigadeführer August Schmidhuber	(January – May 1945)

Second in Command

SS Standartenführer d.R. Stefan Hedrich	(March 1942 – June 1943)

Chief of Staff

SS Hauptsturmführer Erich Eberhardt	(March 1942 – June 1943)
SS Sturmbannführer Herbert Wachsmann	(June 1943 – August 1944)
SS Sturmbannführer Friedrich Christoph	(January – March 1945)
SS Sturmbannführer Josef Sepp Niedermayer	(March – May 1945)

Quartermaster

SS Hauptsturmführer Schmidt	(March 1942 – July 1943)
SS Sturmbannführer Robert Zeller	(July – October 1943)
SS Hauptsturmführer Fritz Greindl	(November 1943 – August 1944)
SS Hauptsturmführer Hannes Richter	(August 1944 – March 1945)